PRAISE FOR T

The next 40 days are going to be life-changing for you! Suzanne DeWitt Hall's Transfigured is a beautiful walk through the Bible and how it connects the LGBTQ+ Community to a loving God. In this time where so many Churches and individual Christian's are rejecting queer people for their identity and orientation, having a resource like this is so important and necessary. Prepare for a journey, emotionally and mentally, and most of all, get ready to be Transfigured.

Megan Hamlin, transgender female, Transgender Rights Advocate and Christian Blogger, she/her/hers.

This devotional stirs up feelings—both affirming and challenging—that can move forward the prayer life of a broken community: Those who are not trans and not intersex may never have thought about these things the way Suzanne has brought them to you here. Those who are gender minorities are relieved for a moment from the nearly thankless, constant work of having to educate, argue with and defend ourselves from those in our own faith family. We can come together here to pray, each as we are, as one community in faith.

Donovan Ackley III, male with an intersex condition, retired Director of Training and Curriculum for Trans Lifeline, he/him/his.

Suzanne has a wonderful way of clearly presenting what is obvious yet often overlooked when reading the scriptures, and is constantly pointing us toward Christ in the devotionals. Her gentle and affirming style is refreshing to read.

Laurie Suzanne Scott, author of *God Doesn't Make Mistakes: Confessions of a Transgender Christian.*

As a non-binary person, having a devotional specifically for myself and other genderqueer and trans people means so much. God is seen in all genders and I am thankful to Suzanne for writing such an important work.

H.L. Holder, Blogger, they/them/theirs.

Transfigured delivers an uplifting and much needed affirming devotional for gender-queer and transgender people. It offers comfort and healing as it unravels the truth from deep within the scriptures. DeWitt Hall's 40 day devotional is a worthy addition to any LGBTQI religious studies library.

Cheryl B. Evans, Author of *What Does God Think? Transgender People and the Bible* and *I Promised Not to Tell: Raising a Transgender Child,* she/her/hers.

Suzanne DeWitt Hall follows her open-hearted devotional Where True Love Is with another collection of devotions stunning in their clarity and compassion. Her short reflections on the beauty of gender diversity—both within the spectrum of humanity, and within the self of God—offer multiple lenses for trans, genderqueer, and other non-gender-conforming people to witness their own stories in the holy books of the Christian faith. Interweaving contemporary understandings of gender with ancient biblical verses, Suzanne demonstrates how our manifold God has been continually working for the inclusion, celebration, and liberation of those too often considered "other." These forty devotions are perfect for personal meditation, or for a group study during Lent or another congregational time for self-reflection and neighborly love.

Rev. Emmy R. Kegler, founder and editor of *Queer Grace*, co-leader of the Queer Grace Community in Minneapolis. Queer woman, she/her/hers.

The church has been dreadfully behind on conversations relating to understanding and embracing our transgender and gender non-conforming siblings, and even within the LGBT+ Christian movement, there have been very few resources that are focused on the needs and experiences of this important community. Suzanne DeWitt Hall's new resource Transfigured is changing that. This devotional is full of powerful meditations and reflections for the trans* and gender queer community as they journey deeper into their own spiritual lives and calls everyone who embarks on this forty-day journey towards a posture of radical authenticity and grounding in our truest selves. I recommend this resource for every faith community that seeks to minister well to their trans* and gender non-conforming members.

Brandan Robertson, Lead Pastor, Missiongathering San Diego, and author of *True Inclusion: Creating Communities of Radical Embrace,* he/him/his.

I will recommend Suzanne DeWitt Hall's book "Transfigured" to every gender-queer and transgender person I know, for it is written for them. I will also recommend it to their friends and families and all allies and everyone else. It's a beautifully and graciously written daily devotional that leads one gently and wisely on a forty day spiritual journey towards self-affirmation and one's rightful place in the Christian family.

David Hayward, aka 'nakedpastor', cartoonist, artist, online community facilitator, life-coach, and author of *The Art of Coming Out*, he/him/his.

Be transfigured by the inclusive love and insights in this 40-day devotional! "Transfigured" is aimed at gender-queer and transgender people, but anyone will be blessed by its liberating scripture-based meditations. Meet "our gender-full God" and the Biblical eunuchs who became "non-binary heroes." Discover how the Bible affirms gender complexity, transformation and freedom. Each day concludes with an inspirational quote from a variety of thinkers, including contemporary trans trailblazers.

Rev. Kittredge Cherry, Founder of Qspirit.net and Jesusinlove.org, author of *Art That Dares: Gay Jesus, Woman Christ, and More*, she/her/hers.

Transfigured is an important devotional guide to contribute to the healing process in response to the Church's insistence on binary gender conformity. Through relevant Scripture, fresh hermenutical comments, and diversely-sourced inspiring quotes, this 40-day devotional holds the power to deepen and widen imagination related to long-held assumptions and inclusion for genderqueer, transgender, gender non-conforming, and cisgender people alike.

Rev. Erica Lea-Simka, pastor, Albuquerque Mennonite Church; contributor to *Our Witness: The Unheard Stories of LGBT+ Christians*, she/her/hers.

With great passion and tenderness, Suzanne's writing offers much-needed embrace, encouragement and affirmation of our LBGTQ brothers and sisters. She invites all of us to expand our minds, hearts and spirits as we follow the One who transcends our categories. I'm grateful for her life-giving words.

Rev. Susan Rogers, Pastor of The Well at Springfield, she/her/hers

If the church is to be truly diverse, one of the most important things we can do is to re-center our interpretation of Scripture so that an LGBTQ-affirming lens might finally be our default lens. Suzanne DeWitt Hall's loving and uplifting words in Transfigured take us another step closer toward that sacred goal. Her devotions are celebrations of a God who loves those whom, like God, may not fit all of the arbitrary labels we have made, and what worthy celebrations they are!

Rev. Eric Atcheson, author of *Oregon Trail Theology: The Frontier Millennial Christians Face—And How We're Ready*, he/him/his.

Geared towards the TQI of the LGBTQI+ community, Suzanne has created a Spirit-inspired daily devotional that will help those most vulnerable in our community understand that God has created them just as they are, in His/Her Image. I encourage Pastors everywhere to order many copies of this new book to be used as Sunday School lessons or Bible Studies for their LGBTQI+ members who want to learn more about the truth of God's love and devotion to them for seeking them as their Lord and Savior just as He/She created them.

Rainbow Pastor David Moorman, HIV Awareness Educator, he/him/his.

Devotionals are intended to enhance or inspire our devotement to God. TRANSFIGURED accomplishes this. Those who have, as yet, only experienced biblical texts as a pelting hail, will experience scripture here as a soft, saturating rain. But this healing compilation of fresh perspectives has a greater work to accomplish. Anyone who is sensitive to, but considers themselves outside of the LGBTQ+ world, eager to understand that world better, will find this work to be an unthreatening immersion into a foreign, fascinating culture. Anyone anywhere who has suffered from a much too small sense of self-worth: this devotional reclaims the power of scripture as a healing salve for our souls. In these pages you will see yourself, at last, as your Kingdom of God self: transfigured right before your eyes.

Richard Hadley, MDiv, BCC, he/him/his.

TRANSFIGURED

A 40-day journey through scripture for gender-queer and transgender people

Volume 2 of the *Where True Love Is* Series

SUZANNE DEWITT HALL

Foreword by

REV. DR. PAULA STONE WILLIAMS

Cover photograph courtesy of JPS/Shutterstock.

DH Strategies
www.ipromotebooks.com

First Edition
Rev. 1.2

ISBN-13: 978-0986408038
ISBN-10: 0986408034

Printed in the United States of America

DEDICATION

There's a bright orange sticky note on the wall of my office which reads "Remember us." I put it up the day my transmasculine spouse Declan described a vision he'd had of devastated LGBTQIA+ young people living on the streets after being kicked out of the homes and lives of their families.

Declan cries nearly every day for the people he saw in that vision. His life is dedicated to advocating for them, and to supporting my work. Without him this book would not exist.

I love you, Declan. All my books are for you, and for those you work so tirelessly to protect. May your prayers for change be answered.

CONTENTS

FOREWORD

I live in the foothills of the Rockies, about 20 miles from Rocky Mountain National Park. I have hiked over 2,500 miles in these majestic mountains, and there is a flow to my routine.

As a day hiker, most of my hikes consist of going up for a few hours, followed by going down for a few hours. The difference is not in variation, but elevation. The Gem Lake Trail rises 1,000 feet before you trudge another 1,000 feet back down. The trail to Long's Peak gains 5,000 feet before reaching its 14,259-foot summit. If you climb Long's, you'll spend at least four or five hours going up, followed by another four or five down. Hiking in the Rockies is pretty simple. First you hike up; then you hike down.

Life is not like hiking in the Rockies. Life is more like hiking on the Appalachian Trail, where a single day may include 10 agonizing climbs followed by an equal number of frustrating descents. You feel like Sisyphus, rolling his proverbial stone. Life provides a steady supply of ups and downs, which is why maintaining a stable center is critically important.

When I came out as transgender, within seven days I lost all of my jobs. I had been the CEO of a large Christian ministry and the editor-at-large of a Christian magazine. I was on the regular preaching team of two mega churches and taught in two different seminaries. It was all gone in seven days. The evangelical world ostracized me, but they could not ostracize my faith. I am now a more committed follower of Jesus than I have ever been.

Jesus did not reject me. Evangelicals did. Of course, you already know that. That is the reason you are reading this book. The Christian world might have given up on you, but you did not give up on nurturing your own spiritual center.

Life is difficult. Whether you are transgender or not, maintaining a stable spiritual center is a challenge. Life will always deliver grueling uphill climbs and slippery descents.

In *Transfigured, a 40-day journey through scripture for gender-queer and transgender people*, Suzanne DeWitt Hall has created a book to take with us on those trails that go up and down 10 times a day. Her devotions provide encouragement, hope, instruction, comfort and solace. Though written for the non-binary and transgender community, any serious trail hiker will benefit from the good work she has done.

The call toward authenticity is holy; it is sacred; it is for the greater good. As you continue on your sacred journey, answering God's call to live authentically, I hope you find strength and comfort from Transfigured. And Suzanne, thank you for giving us centering sustenance for the journey.

Rev. Dr. Paula Stone Williams
Pastor of Preaching and Worship
Left Hand Church
Longmont, Colorado

INTRODUCTION

In writing this book, I hope to help heal a tiny fraction of the harm perpetrated against gender-queer and transgender people in the name of the church.

I've been writing about sexuality and gender issues for a number of years, and have had the honor of forming relationships with a variety of people who have experienced this harm. The stories of exclusion from Christian fellowship, broken marriages, violence, and fear are heartbreaking.

I am cisqueer, and therefore merely an observer of the non-binary gender experience. I can't know what the struggle is like. But I *can* try to make a difference by offering a view of scripture which illustrates the Creator's loving acceptance of God's non-binary and transgender children.

A few devotions in this book were excerpted from volume 1 of the *Where True Love Is* series. Both devotionals center around the following verse:

> *Everyone who loves has been born of God and knows God. Whoever does not love does not know God, because God is love.*
> (1 John 4: 7-8, NIV)

The beloved disciple tells us that God *is* love. John wrote these words because every generation needs to hear them.

You need to hear them.

A famous hymn written by James Quinn called *Here in Christ we Gather* contains the following refrain:

> "God is love, and where true love is
> God himself is there."

The name for the *Where True Love Is* series came from these lyrics. This essential reality—that God is love—permeates every word in this volume.

Transfigured is a 40-day journey you and I go on together; a journey of exploration and transformation. As you read the contemplations offered each day, allow the Spirit who is both love and truth to penetrate your heart and mind, and bring you peace.

May we all be transfigured by the journey.

Pronoun Usage

The question of God's gender is an ongoing theme in this devotional. You will find the following pronouns used throughout the book when referring to persons of the Trinity:

Creator/Father	They/Them/Theirs
Jesus	He/Him/His
Holy Spirit	She/Her/Hers

References to eunuchs also use they/them/theirs pronouns.

BIBLICAL TRANSLATION GUIDE

Objections to the legitimacy of LGBTQIA+ faith are found in widely ranging denominations and traditions. This devotional therefore includes a variety of Bible translations to reflect that diversity. Acronyms for included versions are listed below.

ASV	American Standard Version
CSB	Christian Standard Bible
ESV	English Standard Version
KJV	King James Version
NABRE	New American Bible Revised Edition
NASB	New American Standard Bible
NIV	New International Version
NKJV	New King James Version
NRSV	New Revised Standard Version
NRSVCE	New Revised Standard Version Catholic Edition
RSV	Revised Standard Version

First Things

We begin with a few first things, before moving on to specific areas of focus in our scriptural journey. May the Spirit breathe revelation through these words.

DAY 1:   THE SUBTLE SHIFTING OF GENDER

When I bring clouds over the earth and the bow is seen in the clouds, I will remember my covenant that is between me and you and every living creature of all flesh. (Genesis 9:14-15 NRSVCE)

After the massive flood which Noah survived by building an ark, God promised their anger would not burn so hot so as to result in total annihilation again. The symbol they created for that promise is a rainbow.

The LGBTQIA+ movement chose the rainbow to illustrate the concept of spectrum and variety. Flags and posters include vivid, contrasting stripes. But in God's rainbows, there are no distinct demarcations between violet, indigo, blue, and green. The colors gradually shift from one to the next without our ability to detect where one ends and the next begins. The shift between hues is dissolving and soft.

We sometimes hear the phrase "all the colors of the rainbow," but our ability to perceive color is a tiny subset of the hues which other creatures' eyes can see. Human retinas are limited in their cones and rods, and human minds are just as limited.

Maybe even more so.

The magic of light contains color which no creature can see, not even those with the most complex and specialized visual systems. The Creator alone is witness to the full majesty of the spectrum.

God's palette of shifting hues is vast, subtle, and beyond our comprehension. We humans are like those colors. Subtle, shifting, unique. Non-binary. Unable to be labeled or singled out.

We are all beautiful, one-of-a-kind, and fully seen by God's eyes alone.

The white light streams down to be broken up by those human prisms into all the colors of the rainbow. Take your own color in the pattern and be just that.
Charles R. Brown

DAY 2: WE CAN'T UNDERSTAND THE WORK OF GOD

As you do not know the path of the wind,
or how the body is formed in a mother's womb,
so you cannot understand the work of God,
the Maker of all things.
(Ecclesiastes 11:5 NIV)

Many Christians believe that by knowing the Bible well enough, people become expert in the ways of God. In some cases they feel sanctioned or even anointed by God to proclaim the righteousness or sinfulness of others, based on things like gender presentation or non-binary gender identification.

But today's reading shows us the opposite is true. The passage from Ecclesiastes proclaims that we *cannot* understand the work of God. Not even by studying the Old Testament laws, the warnings of the prophets, or the injunctions in the epistles. The author points out that we especially can't know the mysterious ways in which God weaves together our beings within the womb, in all our wondrous, intricate diversity.

We cannot understand the work of God. But we can rest in the knowledge that our Creator designed each of us to reflect the enormity of God's incomprehensible beauty in a very particular way.

You are God's particular reflection. Now go shine.

Teach thy tongue to say "I do not know," and thou shalt progress.
Maimonides

DAY 3: IN BETWEENS MAKE PEOPLE UNCOMFORTABLE

Can you fathom the mysteries of God? Can you probe the limits of the Almighty? They are higher than the heavens above—what can you do? They are deeper than the depths below—what can you know? Their measure is longer than the earth and wider than the sea.
(Job 11:7-9 NIV)

The Enlightenment led us to believe humans have the ability to comprehend pretty much everything. It also resulted in a demand that all ideas be categorized as correct or incorrect. The idea of in-betweenness has become alien, and existing within it makes us uncomfortable.

When we are uncomfortable, we get anxious and we don't know how to respond. Sometimes that discomfort leads to anger and a desire to make the discomfort stop, even by force. Given this reality, it's no wonder gender is shoved into rigid silos.

In Western cultures it is more comfortable for people to be able to slot humans into two categories where there is no liminal mystery. But other cultures and religions have room for ambiguity in nature, philosophy, and humanity.

Shouldn't we as well? After all, our God is a God of both/and rather than either/or. Jesus was a king yet rode a donkey. Christians believe that victory is achieved through self-donation, right down to dying on a cross. Jesus tells us that the least of us here is the greatest in the kingdom. Our Godhead is a Trinity: a mixture of persons with differing characteristics.

Our God is comfortable with states which are both one thing and also another. Western civilization may not be wholly comfortable yet, but God surely is.

And our God is comfortable with *you*, no matter how much of a gender mix you are.

> *Regarding the whole business of gender, I argue that the paired Genesis creation narratives present gender as our business to explore and to define and not just God's business to declare and to impose.*
>
> Rev. Canon Scott Cowdell

Our Gender-full God

Fathers and doctors of the church like Origen and Augustine recognized that language is too limited to adequately describe God. There are no words which can capture the being which loved so much that it exploded into energy and matter. But humans are designed to seek understanding, and language creates form for incomprehensible concepts, and so we apply human ideas to a God who is not human.

The scriptures were written by men in eras when the idea of masculinity and power went hand in hand. When reading the Bible, it's easy to conclude that God is a man. But how can the force that brought all things into being be constrained by gender? Legalistic Christians demand that biological sex and gender are one and the same. But God doesn't have a body. He created biology, but doesn't inhabit it as we do. So how can God be a man?

The same Christians shout about God not making mistakes, as if God only works in binaries and anything falling outside black and white cannot be from them. But creation is so full of color and variation that it's incomprehensible why any Christian would want to pare God down to the limited palette of our individual expectations.

Over the next week you'll read scriptures which explore the idea of God's gender, and see that the idea of a cis-Creator is absurd.

Our God is gender-full.

DAY 4: MALE AND FEMALE GOD CREATED THEM

Then God said, "Let us make mankind in our image, in our likeness, so that they may rule over the fish in the sea and the birds in the sky, over the livestock and all the wild animals, and over all the creatures that move along the ground." So God created mankind in his own image, in the image of God he created them; male and female he created them.
(Genesis 1:26-27 NIV)

Most of us miss the full import of this passage. We focus on the binary and read it as God having made us male OR female. But the statement is so much more profound than that, because it speaks not only about human gender identity, but about God themself. And that's a biggie.

Read the passage again, but slow down and focus on the last sentence:

So God created mankind in his own image, in the image of God he created them; male and female he created them.

Did you catch it this time? In the image of God they created them, male AND female. It doesn't say "or," it says "and," which tells us *God* is both, and we are not binary.

This may seem like verbal gymnastics, but it truly isn't. Christian LGBTQIA+ critics tout the passage as the definitive indictment of non-conforming gender and sexual identities. Biblical literalists demand we take the words to mean what they say. It is only logical that we should therefore examine the words closely and delve deep into the awesome mystery of God's creation, and of their very being.

The majority of the adult population grew up with traditional concepts of femininity and masculinity, and aligned gender with external sex characteristics. Many schools of Christian thought believe we carry a binary gender when we leave our bodies. But when we are no longer equipped with genitalia, Adam's apples, or bone structure, what will our gender resemble? Will our presences in the mystical state known as heaven be intensified versions of binary genders, or will our spirits broaden to be even more like God? More fully *both*, just as God is both?

When we allow the Holy Spirit to breathe meaning through today's scripture we make a magnificent discovery:

Gender fluid people are actually more God-like than those who identify with a gender binary.

Why isn't God female? As my teacher said, "He is."
Rich Robinson

DAY 5:   THE CREATOR AS BIRTH MOTHER

The Lord goes out like a mighty man, like a man of war he stirs up his zeal; he cries out, he shouts aloud, he shows himself mighty against his foes. For a long time I have held my peace; I have kept still and restrained myself; now I will cry out like a woman in labor; I will gasp and pant.
(Isaiah 42:13–14 ESV)

"Has the rain a father, or who has begotten the drops of dew? From whose womb did the ice come forth, and who has given birth to the frost of heaven? The waters become hard like stone, and the face of the deep is frozen."
(Job 38:28–30 ESV)

"Can a woman [mother] forget her nursing child, that she should have no compassion on the son of her womb? Even these may forget, yet I will not forget you. Behold, I have engraved you on the palms of my hands; your walls are continually before me."
(Isaiah 49:15–16 ESV)

You ignored the Rock who gave you birth; you forgot the God who gave birth to you.
(Deuteronomy 32:18 CSB)

Today's contemplation is unusual in that it centers around passages from several books rather than from a single story. The focus is a concept; that God is described using female language.

In each passage you see a reference to the epitomical act of biological femininity; giving birth. In the first, the Lord's zeal is compared to labor pains. In the second, God's womb is the source of ice and frost. In the third, God's compassion is like that of a nursing mother. In the last, God is described as having given birth to us all.

This is powerful enough without going any further. But there's something special about each of these passages. If you reread them, you will see that these are not the words of prophets describing God's characteristics. They are the words of God themself, self-describing as feminine. And not just a little feminine, but so feminine that they are capable of carrying children, giving birth to children, and nursing children.

10

When we read these words, we should be assured that God has no fear of inclusive language, and no concern about being labeled a gender with which they don't identify.

God themself identifies as female.

Orthodox theology says all human beings are made in the image of God, that God does not have a gender. He encompasses gender – he is both male and female and beyond male and female. So when we only speak of God in the male form, that's actually giving us a deficient understanding of who God is.

Rev Jody Stowell

DAY 6: WISDOM AS A FEMALE JESUS

Do not forsake wisdom, and she will protect you;
love her, and she will watch over you.
Cherish her, and she will exalt you;
embrace her, and she will honor you.
She will give you a garland to grace your head
and present you with a glorious crown."
(Proverbs 4:6,8-9 NIV)

Some of the ancient Fathers and Doctors of the church believed that Wisdom passages like today's referred to Jesus Christ.

Here's why:

"I, wisdom, dwell with prudence, and find out knowledge and discretion. I love those who love me, and those who seek me diligently will find me. I have been established from everlasting, from the beginning, before there was ever an earth. When He prepared the heavens, I was there, when He drew a circle on the face of the deep, when He established the clouds above, when He strengthened the fountains of the deep, when He assigned to the sea its limit, so that the waters would not transgress His command, when He marked out the foundations of the earth, then I was beside Him as a master craftsman; and I was daily His delight, rejoicing always before Him, rejoicing in His inhabited world, and my delight was with the sons of men." (Proverbs 8:12, 17, 23, 27-31 NKJV)

It's easy to read these words and see how they line up with the opening of John's gospel, where we hear that Jesus was with God (and *was* God) from the beginning. We can see it in the way Jesus delighted in the sons of men, then and now.

But what we also see is that Wisdom is frequently described as female. Today's opening scripture is just one example of many verses in which this is the case.

Cultures the world over recognize the life-giving force which created the universes to be both male and female. But Western cultures have a harder time with this. Jesus came into the world as the son of Mary, living life performing the masculine gender of his day.

Because of this, it's hard for many people to embrace the idea of a non-binary Jesus. But when we study Wisdom passages, we find that there is in fact a biblical basis for the idea.

So remember: cherish Wisdom—cherish Jesus—who delights in you, and she will present you with a glorious crown.

> *The only-begotten Son, the Wisdom of God, created the entire universe. Scripture says: You have made all things by your wisdom, and the earth is full of your creatures. Yet simply to be was not enough: God also wanted his creatures to be good. That is why he was pleased that his own wisdom should descend to their level and impress upon each of them singly and upon all of them together a certain resemblance to their Model. It would then be manifest that God's creatures shared in his wisdom and that all his works were worthy of him.*
>
> St. Athanasius

DAY 7: JESUS AS MOTHER HEN

"O Jerusalem, Jerusalem, the city that kills the prophets and stones those who are sent to it! How often would I have gathered your children together as a hen gathers her brood under her wings, and you were not willing!"
(Matthew 23:37 ESV)

When you have a moment, search for videos which show hens sheltering their chicks. As you watch them, you'll see that the mother settles in low to the ground when the wind blows hard or danger comes. The chicks dive beneath her, seeking warmth and shelter from whatever lies outside. When the coast is clear, the tiny creatures pop back out from beneath her wings; balls of hapless fuzz who didn't really understand what the problem had been and were ready to launch themselves back into the dangerous world headlong.

In contrast, roosters are the kings of the flock, bossing the others about, attacking foes (and sometimes friends), and generally being aggressive forces of reckoning.

Jesus had his choice of metaphors to employ as the conclusion to this chapter full of the seven woes he proclaims to the hypocritical scribes and Pharisees. A few sentences before this one, Jesus says:

"You serpents, you brood of vipers, how are you to escape being sentenced to hell?" (Matthew 23:33 ESV)

Clearly, he is not pleased by their behavior. So why didn't he choose the angry, aggressive masculine metaphor of a rooster, rather than the protective feminine nurturance of a mother hen to describe his feelings?

Jesus tells us that his response to outrageous sin is to act as a feminine entity of love.

He invites you to rest in the warmth of that accepting protection.

You can have your king-god. You can have your warrior-god. You can have your father-god. Today, I'm opting for the Mother-Hen-God. The God who welcomes all her children under her wings, no matter how they behave, or how they look, or what annoying and inappropriate things they

14

do. The God who opens her heart of healing. The God who feels what I feel, who validates me as a mother, who assures me that when I have made mistakes, when I have wandered from the right path, and when I have been overwhelmed by the foxes, those holy wings are still spread over me, protecting me, sheltering me, keeping me safe, loving me.

Leah D. Shade

DAY 8:   THE SEX SHIFTING OF EVE AND JESUS

The man gave names to all cattle, and to the birds of the air, and to every animal of the field; but for the man there was not found a helper as his partner. So the Lord God caused a deep sleep to fall upon the man, and he slept; then he took one of his ribs and closed up its place with flesh. And the rib that the Lord God had taken from the man he made into a woman and brought her to the man.

Then the man said, "This at last is bone of my bones and flesh of my flesh; this one shall be called Woman, for out of Man this one was taken."
(Genesis 2:20-23 NRSV)

The teaching of the church from ancient days is that Jesus received his fleshly self from Mary. Scripture also teaches that Jesus is the new Adam, born of the new Eve.

Now Eve is a fascinating creature for many reasons. If we take the Genesis account in its literal meaning, as fundamentalist Christians demand we do, Eve is the first instance of human cloning and also the first shifting of gender. God reached into Adam, pulled out a bit of bone, and grew Eve from Adam's XY DNA so he could have a companion. Eve was created genetically male, and yet transformed into woman.

Then along comes Jesus and the whole pattern is both repeated and reversed. The first couple's refusal to cooperate is turned around by Mary's yes, and the second act of cloning occurs. The Holy Spirit comes upon the second Eve, and the child takes flesh from her and is conceived. Conceived of Mary's flesh. Conceived with XX chromosome pairing. Conceived genetically female, and yet transformed into man.

We don't know what physical miracles took place during the creation of humanity or the conception of Jesus. But we do know that they are extraordinary, miraculous, and potentially illustrate biological sex shifting. This doesn't match the experience of today's transgender people. But the concept of transition seems to have been in play.

A quick look at the dictionary for the prefix "trans" tells us that it means "across," "beyond," "through," and "changing thoroughly," all of which are great terms for the person of Christ. He cuts across all boundaries. He is beyond our understanding. He is through all and in all. He changes us thoroughly into new creations.

In his person, and in his salvific actions, Jesus is truly the first and forever trans man. There in the beginning with God, and with us to the very end.

Deep inside the universe lies the potential of the phenomena of consciousness. The mystery of "you" existed as a potential within the stuff of matter for billions of years, and before that within the infinite sea of consciousness that is God, of which you are a wave. Here you are, birthed out of the ecstatic merging of two others, you are consciousness that learns and grows. You are a child of the universe, a child of the stars, a child of the earth, a child of God, blossomed from love into an infinite love awakening. In all infinite time and possibilities, infinity gave way to you. Here you are.

Jacob. M. Wright

DAY 9:   THE FULL-BREASTED JESUS

And I turned to see the voice that spake with me. And having turned I
saw seven golden candlesticks; and in the midst of the candlesticks one like
unto a son of man, clothed with a garment down to the foot, and girt about
at the breasts with a golden girdle.
(Revelation 1:12-13 ASV)

John's head must have spun with all the visions he experienced as described in the book of Revelation. Some were glorious and many were downright frightening. In today's passage John describes the breasts of the Son of Man. We know it refers to Jesus, because a few verses later this white-haired, fiery-eyed figure explains that he is the first and last, the one who died and rose again.

So what about these breasts?

Many Bible translations replace the term breasts with "chest," but this seems to be out of some sort of squeamishness about a full-breasted Jesus which the author of Revelation didn't share. We can see that the term "chest" isn't an appropriate translation by looking at the Greek word, which is μαστοῖς (mastois). μαστοῖς is used only two other times in the New Testament. The first is in Luke 11:27:

While he was saying this, a woman in the crowd raised her voice and said
to him, "Blessed is the womb that bore you and the breasts that nursed
you!" (NRSV)

The second is Luke 23:29:

For the time will come when you will say, 'Blessed are the childless women,
the wombs that never bore and the breasts that never nursed!' (NIV)

As you can see, both passages clearly refer to breasts which have the capability of producing milk. Female breasts.

In contrast, several other passages use στῆθος (stéthos) for male breasts, for example in Luke 18:13:

But the tax collector, standing some distance away, was even unwilling to
lift up his eyes to heaven, but was beating his breast, saying, 'God, be
merciful to me, the sinner!' (NASB)

Most significantly, John's vision shows us angels who are girded the way Jesus was in chapter 1, and yet this verse contains the Greek word for *male* breasts rather than female:

> *…and there came out from the temple the seven angels that had the seven plagues, arrayed with precious stone, pure and bright, and girt about their breasts with golden girdles.* (Revelation 15:6 ASV)

The book of Revelation is filled with fascinating symbolic imagery. In this case the beloved disciple very clearly wanted readers to view the Son of Man—Jesus Christ—as having the nurturing capability to nurse.

We can't know why John's vision included the feminine detail of breasts nestled within fear- and awe-inspiring imagery. But John *did* include it.

The feminine breasts of Jesus are therefore important, and shouldn't be swept away by confused or scandalized translators.

> *God's ways are higher than our ways not because he is less compassionate than we are but because he is more compassionate than we can ever imagine.*
> Rachel Held Evans

DAY 10: JESUS LIKE US IN ALL WAYS

Since the children have flesh and blood, he too shared in their humanity so that by his death he might break the power of him who holds the power of death—that is, the devil—and free those who all their lives were held in slavery by their fear of death. For surely it is not angels he helps, but Abraham's descendants. For this reason he had to be made like them, fully human in every way, in order that he might become a merciful and faithful high priest in service to God, and that he might make atonement for the sins of the people.
(Hebrews 2:14-17 NIV)

Hebrews is a gorgeous book, filled with rich, liturgical language and deep theological thought. You can almost smell the incense as you read it.

The author reminds us today that Jesus was fully human and like us in all ways. This is a profound thought, and not to be brushed away without examination. If Jesus is like us in all ways, it means he is like us in all our gender and sexual diversity. He is heterosexual, homosexual, bisexual, asexual, male, female, transgender, agender, and intersex. He is every variation imaginable, and then some.

Fully like us.

Fully understanding all the ways in which our unique circumstances pull us into acts both righteous and foul, having experienced the tug himself.

Jesus is the one in whom you can place your trust, no matter how you identify. Jesus, our non-binary God. Jesus, whose pronouns might be he/him/his, but who we know to be more.

Jesus, like you in every way, is the one who will be your judge.

What he's been creating, since the first beat of your heart, is a living, breathing, priceless work of art.
Steven Curtis Chapman

BIOLOGICAL SEX AND GENDER

Poor Adam and Eve; they bear the brunt of so many modern Christian claims about sexuality and gender. But in the garden, they lived in blissful ignorance that there was anything to be arguing over. Both of them were simply wholly themselves; male and female, as God is male and female.

But then that dratted serpent came along, pointing out separation and differences, and everything changed.

Over the next few days you'll examine the idea of a gender binary so we can return to that garden state of simple acceptance.

DAY 11:   NAKEDNESS IS NOT A PROBLEM

The man and his wife were both naked, yet they felt no shame.
(Genesis 2:25 NABRE)

This passage shows us God's design is for nakedness to not be shameful, yet look what happens:

> *The woman saw that the tree was good for food and pleasing to the eyes, and the tree was desirable for gaining wisdom. So she took some of its fruit and ate it; and she also gave some to her husband, who was with her, and he ate it. Then the eyes of both of them were opened, and they knew that they were naked; so they sewed fig leaves together and made loincloths for themselves. When they heard the sound of the Lord God walking about in the garden at the breezy time of the day, the man and his wife hid themselves from the Lord God among the trees of the garden. The Lord God then called to the man and asked him: Where are you? He answered, "I heard you in the garden; but I was afraid, because I was naked, so I hid."*
> (Genesis 3:6-10 NABRE)

We are trained from an early age to cover up our nakedness. Our parents squawk if we traipse out of our bedrooms clad only in a diaper when a neighbor pops over to visit. The message is reinforced as the years pass, and we find that being stripped of clothes makes us feel exposed, vulnerable, and embarrassed.

As we move from childhood to adolescence and the teen years, we discover that nakedness isn't limited to just a lack of clothing. We learn to cover up all sorts of things rather than risk exposure from too close a look at our true selves. Some of us learn to use language patterns and mannerisms which match the gender performance people expect from us, even though they feel unnatural, like having to wear the hair shirts described in Old Testament scriptures. Some of us find the thought of exposure to be so overwhelming that we'd rather die than be found out or continue wearing a persona that is a sham.

The insidious snake in that ancient garden convinced Adam and Eve that nakedness was something to be hidden. Even from God. How ludicrous a thought, and how devious the lies promoted by the forces of darkness. God loves us in all our naked vulnerability. They love us *best* when we return to the state of our own Eden, stripped of every vestige of hiding, when we are most truly ourselves. Just as God created us to be.

Don't think you have to hide from God. They see you. And they love you, especially when you are completely naked.

> *Children are not born knowing what it means to be a boy or a girl; they learn it from their parents, older children and others around them. This learning process begins early. As soon as the doctor announces—based on observing the newborn's external sex organs—"it's a boy" or "it's a girl," the world around a child begins to teach these lessons.*
> Human Rights Campaign

DAY 12: GENDER IDENTIFICATION IN THE TALMUD

When God created mankind, he made them in the likeness of God. He
created them male and female and blessed them.
(Genesis 5:1-2 NIV)

Today we look to the Jewish roots of our faith. The Talmud is an ancient collection of 63 tractates which instructed Jews on how to live. One of the tractates talks about the intersection of biological sex and gender performance, and lists these four categories in addition to male and female:

Androgynos: a person whose external sex characteristics are both male and female.

Tumtum: a person whose external sex characteristics are hidden or unclear.

Aylonit: a biological female who hasn't started to look "womanly" by the time she is 20.

Saris: a biological male who hasn't started to look "manly" by the time he is 20.

These descriptions are driven by body parts rather than identity. The system was developed because gender rules for behavior were closely connected to whether a person was biologically male or female. The Old Testament is filled with rules for male and female behavior.

Here's one example for how gender assignment played out:

Blowing a shofar and listening to the sound was an important part of some religious rituals. Males were allowed to blow it for everyone to hear. Androgynos could blow it only for other androgynos to hear. Tumtum could blow it only for themselves to hear.

As with Christianity, most of these rules are no longer followed by many Jewish congregations. But at the time of writing, the Jewish faithful recognized that biological sex and gender were non-binary and had to find a way for non-binary people to know what they could and couldn't do. Judaism is the religion out of which Christianity sprang.

It held rules and law to be intrinsically connected to righteousness, yet understood the reality of biological variety. Isn't it odd that our modern version of rules-driven Christianity can't accept that reality?

The more we let God take us over, the more truly ourselves we become — because He made us. He invented us. He invented all the different people that you and I were intended to be.

C.S. Lewis

Day 13: The Bride of Christ is Male and Female

I wish you would bear with me in a little foolishness. Do bear with me! I feel a divine jealousy for you, for I betrothed you to Christ to present you as a pure bride to her one husband.
(2 Corinthians 11:1-2 RSV)

Paul's letters are used by many legalistic Christians to proclaim the sinfulness of non-cisgender identity (as well as non-hetero sexual orientation). But this seems rather odd, given the view of the church Paul conveys in today's passage, and in this one:

Wherefore, my brethren, ye also are become dead to the law by the body of Christ; that ye should be married to another, even to him who is raised from the dead, that we should bring forth fruit unto God.
(Romans 7:4 KJV)

Paul suggests that the church is the bride of Christ. This was not a new concept. The Hebrew Scriptures are replete with comparisons of Israel as an unfaithful wife whom God repeatedly takes back. The Song of Songs weaves a sumptuous, sensuous tapestry of ardent love between God and God's people. So Paul is really continuing a theme, though stating it more tangibly given the physicality which Jesus exhibited.

But both males and females comprise the church, as do those in between.

Paul is describing a feminine unit, the church, which includes masculine members. His language acknowledges a body which can be simultaneously masculine and feminine, male and female. Today's passages come from letters written to two different churches, which would likely have been initially read by the male leaders in those places. Yet Paul tells these males that they are Christ's bride.

Paul reassures us all—cisgender, transgender, and every gender identity and expression in the spectrum—that we are to consider ourselves Jesus' bride.

Don't let anyone tell you your gender is a disqualification.

Novelty comes about by the self-organizing dynamism inherent in creatures themselves. Evolution over deep time is so creative because the material of the world itself has the God-given inner ability to become ever more.

Elizabeth A. Johnson

DAY 14: THE COMPLEXITY OF BIOLOGICAL SEX

"Haven't you read," he replied, "that at the beginning the Creator 'made them male and female,'" (Matthew 19:4 NIV)

When Jesus was confronted by Pharisees who tried to trick him with questions about divorce, he quoted a Genesis creation account in order to illustrate the one-ness of spirit which should come about through marriage. But modern day Pharisees use Jesus' words as a demand for a gender binary, which takes the passage out of context and perverts its meaning.

Demanding that God works only in binaries isn't merely sad, it also flies in the face of actual facts. There are at least five scientifically identifiable biological sexes, though Christian traditionalists want to force gender to correspond with only the first two:

1. People who are born with XX chromosomes and have female sex characteristics.
2. People who are born with XY chromosomes and have male sex characteristics.
3. People who are born with XX chromosomes and have male sex characteristics.
4. People who are born with XY chromosomes and have female sex characteristics.
5. People who are born with mosaic genetics, so that some cells contain XX chromosomes and others contain XY. Sexual characteristics for these people vary.

This list is hardly exhaustive. There are also people whose external genitalia appear to be male while the internal organs are female, and vice versa. Brain differences introduce further diversity into the sex and gender spectrum. The presence or absence of testosterone levels during gestation impacts "femininity" and "masculinity" as understood by culture and as understood by the individual themselves.

The result of all this is effulgent diversity.

God created Adam and Eve male and female. Sometimes they create people at the ends of the male/female spectrum. And sometimes they create them in the middle, where the "and" exists.

What's happening outside church walls is happening inside church walls. It is all part of the human experience. Ignorance and lack of education about sex, sexual orientation, gender identities, and human sexuality in general have led to harmful assumptions and poor pastoral counsel.

Kathy Baldock

Non-Binary Heroes: Eunuchs in the Bible

The closest thing we have in scripture to today's understanding of non-binary and transgender people are eunuchs. The Bible contains numerous references to eunuchs, none of which were ever condemned for simply being who they were.

In this focus area you'll explore passages about eunuchs to show how scripture describes God's view of those who were not cisgender in the days of the prophets and of Jesus.

NOTE: Pronouns for eunuchs are they/them/theirs.

DAY 15: E'BED-MEL'ECH: SAVIOR OF JEREMIAH

*So they took Jeremiah and cast him into the cistern of Malchi'ah, the
king's son, which was in the court of the guard, letting Jeremiah down by
ropes. And there was no water in the cistern, but only mire, and Jeremiah
sank in the mire.*

*When E'bed-mel'ech the Ethiopian, a eunuch, who was in the king's
house, heard that they had put Jeremiah into the cistern—the king was
sitting in the Benjamin Gate— E'bed-mel'ech went from the king's house
and said to the king, "My lord the king, these men have done evil in all
that they did to Jeremiah the prophet by casting him into the cistern; and
he will die there of hunger, for there is no bread left in the city." Then the
king commanded E'bed-mel'ech, the Ethiopian, "Take three men with
you from here, and lift Jeremiah the prophet out of the cistern before he
dies." So E'bed-mel'ech took the men with him and went to the house of
the king, to a wardrobe of the storehouse, and took from there old rags and
worn-out clothes, which he let down to Jeremiah in the cistern by ropes.
Then E'bed-mel'ech the Ethiopian said to Jeremiah, "Put the rags and
clothes between your armpits and the ropes." Jeremiah did so. Then they
drew Jeremiah up with ropes and lifted him out of the cistern. And
Jeremiah remained in the court of the guard.*

*The word of the Lord came to Jeremiah while he was shut up in the court of
the guard: "Go, and say to E'bed-mel'ech the Ethiopian, 'Thus says the Lord
of hosts, the God of Israel: Behold, I will fulfil my words against this city for
evil and not for good, and they shall be accomplished before you on that day.
But I will deliver you on that day, says the Lord, and you shall not be given
into the hand of the men of whom you are afraid. For I will surely save you,
and you shall not fall by the sword; but you shall have your life as a prize of
war, because you have put your trust in me, says the Lord.'"*
(Jeremiah 38:6-13, 39:15-18 RSV)

Our scripture for today is unusually long, but all the verses are
necessary for examining the story. The princes of the land had heard
Jeremiah's dire proclamations of what was to come, and didn't like it.
They decide to put him to death, but luckily, the cistern into which
he was thrown was empty so he didn't drown. Then enters our hero,
E'bed-mel'ech, a eunuch who steps in to save the day. The eunuch talks

to the king, who orders the prophet's release, and then take ropes to pull Jeremiah up and out of the below-ground water tank.

Here's where the details get interesting:

Not only was the eunuch focused on saving Jeremiah's life, E'bed-mel'ech also cared about how comfortable the prophet would be while being excavated. They stop to gather old clothes and rags from the storehouse, and tell Jeremiah how to pad himself so the ropes won't scrape his skin on the way up.

This detail conveys a level of care and tenderness that goes above and beyond the mere call to rescue a dying man. They didn't have to stop for padding. Comfort didn't need to cross E'bed-mel'ech's mind. If they'd simply hoisted Jeremiah up, rope burns and all, they would still go down in biblical history as a hero. But they *did* care how Jeremiah's armpits would handle the rubbing cordage.

The Creator noticed the eunuch's tenderness. God promised E'bed-mel'ech protection during the war that was to come. Some ancient legends even say the eunuch joined Enoch and Elijah in ascending to heaven without tasting death.

E'bed-mel'ech put their trust in God, walked in trust because of that faith, and now rejoices with the Holy Trinity in heaven. We can all be like them in that trust, no matter how our gender identity or performance is manifested.

Let's stop "tolerating" or "accepting" difference, as if we're so much better for not being different. Instead, let's celebrate difference, because in this world it takes a lot of guts to be different and to act differently.

Kate Bornstein

"Let the king appoint overseers in all the provinces of his kingdom that they may gather every beautiful young virgin to the citadel of Susa, to the harem, into the custody of Hegai, the king's eunuch, who is in charge of the women; and let their cosmetics be given them. Then let the young lady who pleases the king be queen in place of Vashti." And the matter pleased the king, and he did accordingly.

So it came about when the command and decree of the king were heard and many young ladies were gathered to the citadel of Susa into the custody of Hegai, that Esther was taken to the king's palace into the custody of Hegai, who was in charge of the women. Now the young lady pleased him and found favor with him. So he quickly provided her with her cosmetics and food, gave her seven choice maids from the king's palace and transferred her and her maids to the best place in the harem.

Now when the turn of Esther, the daughter of Abihail the uncle of Mordecai who had taken her as his daughter, came to go in to the king, she did not request anything except what Hegai, the king's eunuch who was in charge of the women, advised. And Esther found favor in the eyes of all who saw her. So Esther was taken to King Ahasuerus to his royal palace in the tenth month which is the month Tebeth, in the seventh year of his reign. The king loved Esther more than all the women, and she found favor and kindness with him more than all the virgins, so that he set the royal crown on her head and made her queen instead of Vashti.
(Esther 2:3-4, 8-9, 15-17 NASB)

In today's story, the king's wife Vashti refuses to respond to his summons, and because he is embarrassed in front of his guests, the king decides to replace her with a young virgin. Officials are sent throughout the countryside to gather up all the pretty girls, including a young Jewish woman named Esther. Through a complex series of events, Esther later saves the Hebrew people from a holocaust the king proclaimed without realizing she was one of them. Esther's uncle points out that she was called "for such a time as this."

But Esther isn't the only person in the story who had a special calling to save the Jewish people. Hegai, the eunuch who was in charge of the king's women, was instrumental in the whole adventure. Hegai gave Esther choice morsels of food, the best digs in the house, and makeup. They also offered her advice about what the king might like just before she went in to see him.

Hegai's preferential treatment yielded good results: Esther is made queen, and is therefore able to influence the king when an evil man channels his personal vendetta into a plot to wipe out the Jewish people.

Esther rose up and did what needed to be done in order to save the Jews. But without Hegai's ministrations and advice, she might not have been selected to become queen.

Esther was called for such a time as that. But so was the non-binary personage of Hegai.

I was born into a man's body. I wanted to become a woman. This sometimes gives me the feeling of being able to understand both sexes deeply. The suffering I have crossed has increased my spirituality, I believe. And also my ability to intercept the pain of others.
Vladimir Luxuria

DAY 17: THE EUNUCH'S TENDER LOVE OF DANIEL

But Daniel purposed in his heart that he would not defile himself with the portion of the king's meat, nor with the wine which he drank: therefore he requested of the prince of the eunuchs that he might not defile himself. Now God had brought Daniel into favour and tender love with the prince of the eunuchs. And the prince of the eunuchs said unto Daniel, I fear my lord the king, who hath appointed your meat and your drink: for why should he see your faces worse liking than the children which are of your sort? Then shall ye make me endanger my head to the king. Then said Daniel to Melzar, whom the prince of the eunuchs had set over Daniel, Hananiah, Mishael, and Azariah, Prove thy servants, I beseech thee, ten days; and let them give us pulse to eat, and water to drink. Then let our countenances be looked upon before thee, and the countenance of the children that eat of the portion of the king's meat: and as thou seest, deal with thy servants. So he consented to them in this matter, and proved them ten days. And at the end of ten days their countenances appeared fairer and fatter in flesh than all the children which did eat the portion of the king's meat.
(Daniel 1:8-15 KJV)

Esther's story isn't the only one in which we read of special relationships between eunuchs and faith heroes. In today's passage we find Daniel, taken as a child captive into Babylon by King Nebuchadnezzar. The king's plan was to fatten up all the young Israelite noblemen they'd brought for service in the royal court by feeding them special rations of food and wine. As with Esther's story, preparations were extensive. Daniel and his fellow captives were to be educated for three years. Unlike Esther, Daniel requests the eunuch charged with his care to bring food which would not violate Jewish dietary laws.

What we see in these verses is that this non-binary person, the prince of the eunuchs, respected Daniel's request to honor God in the ways he thought he should. The eunuch did this even though it put them at risk of losing their very life.

Not only that; the scriptures say it was through God's power that the eunuch came to favor and love Daniel tenderly.

Clearly God didn't find the Prince of the eunuchs to be morally reprehensible. God worked through them.

Though some in the Christian community do not yet accept that a person who has always tried to conform to what appears to their birth gender can fail at that, we could instead find guidance in the Bible that God's boundless, loving grace and infinite creativity goes well beyond the human cultural constraints regarding gender that we tend to impose on each other. Living enslaved to others' cultural expectations is not required of us in Christ. We are free, even empowered, to be fully ourselves in Christ as God made us - fully human, more (not less) than the social roles of gender, race, class, and religion within which we sometimes confine each other.

Donovan W. Ackley III

DAY 18: THE EUNUCH WHO DESIRES BAPTISM

Now an angel of the Lord said to Philip, "Rise and go toward the south to the road that goes down from Jerusalem to Gaza." This is a desert place. And he rose and went. And there was an Ethiopian, a eunuch, a court official of Candace, queen of the Ethiopians, who was in charge of all her treasure. He had come to Jerusalem to worship and was returning, seated in his chariot, and he was reading the prophet Isaiah. And the Spirit said to Philip, "Go over and join this chariot." So Philip ran to him and heard him reading Isaiah the prophet and asked, "Do you understand what you are reading?" And he said, "How can I, unless someone guides me?" And he invited Philip to come up and sit with him.

Then Philip opened his mouth, and beginning with this Scripture he told him the good news about Jesus. And as they were going along the road they came to some water, and the eunuch said, "See, here is water! What prevents me from being baptized?" And he commanded the chariot to stop, and they both went down into the water, Philip and the eunuch, and he baptized him. And when they came up out of the water, the Spirit of the Lord carried Philip away, and the eunuch saw him no more, and went on his way rejoicing.
(Acts 8:26-31, 35-39 ESV)

What an exciting tale this is! The imagery is vivid: an Ethiopian person studies scripture while riding in a royal chariot, the way we might read a novel on a long drive. Owning scrolls of scripture was no small thing, and it can't have been easy reading given the bumps of wooden or iron-clad wheels across cobbled streets and mud ruts. Phillip must have been quite surprised by what he found when he followed the Spirit's instructions to join them.

Despite their lofty position within the queen's court, the eunuch demonstrates humility in admitting they can't truly understand the words of Isaiah. And when Phillip tells the good news, they are quick to respond, requesting baptism so they could embrace this new thing Jesus promised.

Phillip baptizes the eunuch as requested. He could find no reason not to baptize them, despite their non-binary status.

Once the baptism is complete, Phillip is carried away by the Spirit (which must have blown the eunuch's mind).

The eunuch surely carried their excitement back to Ethiopia, sharing the gospel message and explaining what they'd experienced; becoming an exuberant, non-binary evangelist.

It seems odd that despite the power of this passage and the important role the Ethiopian held within their country's royal court, the eunuch remains unnamed. But perhaps the lack of a name is a good thing. By remaining nameless, we can all become this non-binary person who hungers for God, and for whom Philip can find no reason to refuse baptism.

> *There have always been transgender and gender non-conforming people. There will always be trans and gender non-conforming people. Trans and gender non-conforming people turn up in every culture and every population. In fact, the first gentile Christian in the Book of Acts was someone who could be viewed as gender non-conforming—the Ethiopian Eunuch.*
>
> Vivian Taylor

DAY 19: GOD'S PROMISE TO NON-BINARY BELIEVERS

This is what the Lord says: "Maintain justice and do what is right, for my salvation is close at hand and my righteousness will soon be revealed. Blessed is the one who does this—the person who holds it fast, who keeps the Sabbath without desecrating it, and keeps their hands from doing any evil." Let no foreigner who is bound to the Lord say, "The Lord will surely exclude me from his people." And let no eunuch complain, "I am only a dry tree." For this is what the Lord says: "To the eunuchs who keep my Sabbaths, who choose what pleases me and hold fast to my covenant—to them I will give within my temple and its walls a memorial and a name better than sons and daughters; I will give them an everlasting name that will endure forever.
(Isaiah 56:1-5, NIV)

Christians frequently quote the prophet Isaiah's calls for repentance and predictions of the Messiah to come. But Isaiah also speaks about what things will be like in the future days of restoration and glory.

We can see from today's passage that foreigners and eunuchs may not have felt the same hope those we call the "chosen people" did. There was obviously fear that being "other" would exclude them from God's promises, simply due to that otherness.

But the passage continues on to show us God's response to this thinking. We read about the call for justice, for relationship with God, and for fighting against our internal desires toward selfishness. We also read about the reward to non-binary people who strive for these things. To these people, God promises not merely a place at God's table, but a name "better than sons and daughters." A special place, and a special reward, above that given to those who may believe they have more right to God's blessing.

So let's all strive for what pleases God, and hold fast to the promises of Jesus Christ. In doing so we are given an everlasting name which endures forever.

A name which means "beloved."

> *Every creature is a divine word because it proclaims God.*
> St. Bonaventure

DAY 20: JESUS ACKNOWLEDGES NON-BINARY REALITY

But He said to them, "Not all men can accept this statement, but only those to whom it has been given. For there are eunuchs who were born that way from their mother's womb; and there are eunuchs who were made eunuchs by men; and there are also eunuchs who made themselves eunuchs for the sake of the kingdom of heaven. He who is able to accept this, let him accept it." (Matthew 19:11-12 NASB)

Many traditionalist Christians of our day claim there is no gender spectrum. Matthew's account of Jesus' words, however, proves that claim to be unbiblical. In today's passage, we see Jesus describing three variations of non-binary personhood.

The variations are an important detail. In wrapping up the discussion on marriage which precedes these verses, Jesus could have simply said that some people may not want to marry. Instead, he points out that there are variants in gender even within the masculine category of eunuch.

In the first case, he mentions people with ambiguous genitalia. In the second, he lists the altering of genitalia (which in that day was most likely done as an act of violence). In the third, he leaves genitals out of it, but acknowledges non-binary gender performance.

Because of this description, intersex people can see themselves in his words. Transgender people undergoing gender affirmation surgery can feel acknowledged. And people who perform gender differently than our culture currently expects can find acceptance in his sight.

Jesus concludes by pointing out that many people can't accept what he is trying to tell them. Nothing has changed on this front since the days Jesus roamed the earth. Christians still have trouble believing that he really meant the free gift of his saving love through faith, regardless of a believer's gender identity or expression.

In a world where trans people are demeaned, excluded, exoticized, invalidated, legislated against, and killed—the courage it takes for trans people to live fully into who they are is worthy of respect and honor. I dare say it is a holy act.

Angela Yarber

CLOTHING, HAIR CUTS, AND ADORNMENTS

Clothing is one of the most visible culturally defined gender indicators, and while it has absolutely nothing to do with gender identity, it's a big issue within fundamentalist Christian circles. Arguments launched at non-binary and transgender people often include Bible passages intended to be convincing proofs that their gender performance is somehow making God upset.

Throughout the next few days we examine scripture which deals with clothing to prove the idea is a shallow understanding of both the scriptural texts, and of God themself.

DAY 21: HOW GOD JUDGES EXTERNAL APPEARANCE

But the LORD said to Samuel, "Do not look on his appearance or on the height of his stature, because I have rejected him; for the LORD sees not as man sees; man looks on the outward appearance, but the LORD looks on the heart."
(1 Samuel 16:7 RSV)

Sometimes you have to explore biblical passages deeply to get to their meaning, and sometimes the truth is right there, front and center. Today's verse from 1 Samuel is one of the latter.

In this story, God has sent the prophet Samuel to visit Jesse, because God chose one of Jesse's sons to replace Saul as king over Israel. Jesse parades seven sons past Samuel, who was waiting for God's word about who was the chosen one. A son named Eli'ab was impressive in looks and height, and so Samuel assumes he must be the anointed one. The verse above is God's correction of Samuel's thinking. God didn't choose the person who looked the part. They chose the youngest of the siblings, who apparently was not terribly tall.

That young person was David, someone the scriptures call a man after God's own heart; beloved of God, and ancestor to Jesus.

Transgender people often have stages (before, during, and after transition) in which they don't particularly like how they look. Our culture fetishizes appearance, and non-binary people can feel particularly burdened by societal expectations of gender presentation and performance. But today's passage should offer you comfort, because no matter what people conclude about you in the grocery store or at the gas station, you can rest in the knowledge that the Lord sees you beyond all external characteristics.

God knows the very heart of you. God loves you, just as you have been created, and has called you to a purpose which makes profound use of that wonderful creation. In accepting this reality, we can all be like David: a person after God's own heart.

When our lives are focused on God, awe and wonder lead us to worship God, filling our inner being with a fullness we would never have thought possible. Awe prepares the way in us for the power of God to transform us and this transformation of our inner attitudes can only take place when awe leads us in turn to wonder, admiration, reverence, surrender, and obedience toward God.

James Houston

DAY 22: CLOTHE YOURSELVES WITH CHRIST

So in Christ Jesus you are all children of God through faith, for all of you who were baptized into Christ have clothed yourselves with Christ. There is neither Jew nor Gentile, neither slave nor free, nor is there male and female, for you are all one in Christ Jesus. If you belong to Christ, then you are Abraham's seed, and heirs according to the promise.
(Galatians 3:26-29 NIV)

Christianity is at crisis because so many socially conservative people cling with fear to an understanding of the Bible as a lifeline to God, which if examined too closely will fall apart and leave them drowning in a tide of uncertainty. They demand their long-held views of LGBTQIA+ sinfulness are not only scriptural fact, but are the very glue which holds our society together.

What a terrible and terrifying thing it must be to have a faith that is so tenuously built on a book. It's no wonder they are frightened to question the beliefs they've been taught, when their faith is based not on God themself, but on stories *about* God.

How sweet therefore are today's words from Paul in his letter to the Galatians? They should be sweet indeed to fear-driven Christians who sometimes strike out at the queer community. Their faith journeys could be so much simpler, purer, and driven by love if they could accept what Paul is saying here.

Paul tells us there should be no distinctions. He says we shouldn't label people so they fit into a manufactured hierarchy of power and discrimination. He tells us that in the Kingdom, these things do not exist.

If fear didn't stop legalistic Christians from being honest with themselves, they might even recognize something that isn't stated outright in these words, but which nevertheless is connoted. Paul tells us that heirs of the promise are without race, class, or gender. This *should* mean non-binary people are already a step ahead of the rest of us in understanding what it is that God has in mind for humanity.

Please pray this reality begins to penetrate the hearts of all fear-driven Christians.

> *There are two ways to interpret what Paul says in Galatians 3:28 about our being one in Christ: either it means that we're all whitewashed and homogenized and our differences are erased... or it means that we're called to find a way to make our different identities fit together, like the bright shards in assorted colors that make up the stained glass windows of a cathedral. Are we called to sameness, or are we called to oneness?*
>
> Austen Hartke

DAY 23: THE INTERDEPENDENCE OF MASCULINITY AND FEMININITY

Every man who prays or prophesies with his head covered dishonors his head, but every wife who prays or prophesies with her head uncovered dishonors her head, since it is the same as if her head were shaven. For if a wife will not cover her head, then she should cut her hair short. But since it is disgraceful for a wife to cut off her hair or shave her head, let her cover her head.

Nevertheless, in the Lord woman is not independent of man nor man of woman; for as woman was made from man, so man is now born of woman. And all things are from God. Judge for yourselves: is it proper for a wife to pray to God with her head uncovered? Does not nature itself teach you that if a man wears long hair it is a disgrace for him, but if a woman has long hair, it is her glory? For her hair is given to her for a covering.
(1 Corinthians 11:4-6, 11-15 ESV)

Today's passage is rather confusing, with its demand that a woman who doesn't want to cover her head should shave it, but then a turnabout proclamation that a shaved head is a disgrace.

One obvious question from reading it is why so few denominations follow this teaching, given that biblical-literalists claim we are to continue applying every line of scripture to our faith today?

You can add the passage to your arsenal of examples of disregarded instructions, but the fact that it's ignored isn't the focus of today's devotion. We'll set aside the absurd idea that hair length correlates to holiness, and look instead at the gold buried in the center of the passage:

Nevertheless, in the Lord woman is not independent of man nor man of woman; for as woman was made from man, so man is now born of woman. And all things are from God.

It's unlikely Paul intended to address the beautiful integration and intermingling of gender when he wrote these words. But this is an example of the Holy Spirit breathing through an author. He wrote about women's hair back then, and the Spirit whispered something for *you* to read and relish, right now. She knew you'd move through the instructions to the Corinthians, rebelling against the ideas Paul conveys about gender performance, and then settle in to this affirmation with a sigh of relief.

Femininity is not independent of masculinity, the Spirit says. A woman was made from a man, and a man comes out of a woman. Sometimes that happens at birth, and sometimes it happens later in life.

Through these words, the Spirit tells us there is no independence of gender. We are all a beautiful, interrelated, sometimes messy mix.

Given Paul's warnings about haircuts, jewelry, and women speaking during worship, he was probably uncomfortable with holy messiness.

But God sure isn't.

What does it mean to be transgender? What does it mean to be male or female? I really don't know. But I do know what it means to be human. It is to understand the interconnectedness of us all....I am committed to walking in the shoes of all the people God brings into my life, to see life through their lens. It's hard work, but after so many have done the same for me, how could I choose to live any other way?
Paula Stone Williams

DAY 24: DEUTERONOMY ON CROSS-DRESSING

A woman shall not wear a man's garment, nor shall a man put on a woman's cloak, for whoever does these things is an abomination to the Lord your God.
(Deuteronomy 22:5 ESV)

At the time of Deuteronomy's writing, cultic temple worship included cross-dressing. Men wearing colorful female clothing could be found in the temples of Astarte, Ashtaroth, or Venus, and armor-clad women could be found worshipping Mars.

The Hebrew Scriptures are saturated with the problems and pitfalls of turning away from Yahweh, so it's logical that instructions for faithful Jewish life would include warnings against cross-dressing because of its cultural connection to idolatry.

Inclusion of the term "abomination" underscores the connection to idol worship. If you check a concordance for the term and review the list of verses which include it, you will quickly see its intrinsic coupling with the worship of other gods.

In other words, the author of Deuteronomy wasn't concerned about which robe was for females, and which was for males. (After all, everyone wore dresses). The author was concerned about faithfulness and not misleading others into thinking they were turning away from God.

Even if this wasn't the case, let's look at a few more instructions about clothing from the same chapter:

You shall not wear cloth of wool and linen mixed together. "You shall make yourself tassels on the four corners of the garment with which you cover yourself. (Deuteronomy 22:11-12 ESV)

How many of the Christians you know who preach Deuteronomy 22:5 actually check the fabric content of their clothing so that they don't offend God? How many do you see sporting tassels on their coats?

It's hypocritical to say that one set of injunctions about dress should be adhered to strictly, while completely disregarding additional instructions which appear just six verses later.

If Jesus came to bring abundant life to all who follow him, that means that transgender Christians should be able to stop spending every single bit of their energy defending themselves against those 'clobber passages,' in order to concentrate instead on becoming better disciples. We should be able to move from survival practices to thriving faith. Jesus didn't come to make things marginally more bearable. He came to give us abundant and eternal life.

Austen Hartke

DAY 25: OUTWARD ADORNING

Whose adorning let it not be that outward adorning of plaiting the hair, and of wearing of gold, or of putting on of apparel; But let it be the hidden man of the heart, in that which is not corruptible, even the ornament of a meek and quiet spirit, which is in the sight of God of great price. For after this manner in the old time the holy women also, who trusted in God, adorned themselves.

Finally, be ye all of one mind, having compassion one of another, love as brethren, be pitiful, be courteous: Not rendering evil for evil, or railing for railing: but contrariwise blessing; knowing that ye are thereunto called, that ye should inherit a blessing. For he that will love life, and see good days, let him refrain his tongue from evil, and his lips that they speak no guile: Let him eschew evil, and do good; let him seek peace, and ensue it. For the eyes of the Lord are over the righteous, and his ears are open unto their prayers: but the face of the Lord is against them that do evil.
(1 Peter 3:3-5a, 8-12 KJV)

The King James translation of this passage offers an intermixing of gender, starting out by describing how women should present themselves and then turning to point to the hidden man of the heart. But that's not the important part of today's message.

We've all seen plenty of Christians who wear their hair braided, sport expensive clothes, and glimmer with gold necklaces, earrings, and watches. You can easily find them in church; even in the most socially conservative denominations.

Modern-day Christians have been able to sift through these epistolary instructions to get to the meat of the message. We have no problem recognizing that if the inner adorning is right with God, the outward doesn't matter. If we stop our tongues from doing evil, seek peace, tell the truth, and do good, we can wear what we want.

What traditionalist Christians miss from these passages is that the concept of adornment goes deeper than just hair arrangement and jewelry. They should also recognize that when the "hidden man of the heart" is in right relationship with God, the exterior expression of gender just doesn't matter.

Let's pray these Christians realize that the ears of the Lord are open to the prayers of all, regardless of biological sex, gender identification, or gender performance.

Frankly, I'm not responsible for other people's perceptions and what they consider real or fake. We must abolish the entitlement that deludes us into believing that we have the right to make assumptions about people's identities and project those assumptions onto their genders and bodies.

Janet Mock

DAY 26: SHOW NO PARTIALITY BASED ON DRESS

My brothers, show no partiality as you hold the faith in our Lord Jesus Christ, the Lord of glory. For if a man wearing a gold ring and fine clothing comes into your assembly, and a poor man in shabby clothing also comes in, and if you pay attention to the one who wears the fine clothing and say, "You sit here in a good place," while you say to the poor man, "You stand over there," or, "Sit down at my feet," have you not then made distinctions among yourselves and become judges with evil thoughts?

If you really fulfill the royal law according to the Scripture, "You shall love your neighbor as yourself," you are doing well. But if you show partiality, you are committing sin and are convicted by the law as transgressors. For whoever keeps the whole law but fails in one point has become guilty of all of it.

(James 2:1-4, 8-10 ESV)

For many non-binary and transgender people, walking into a church is a very uncomfortable experience. The anticipation of reactions you might receive can be enough to keep you from going in at all.

The situation is similar to what we see described in today's passage from James. In it, the early Christians treated people differently based on what sort of clothing they wore. Worse, they made distinctions among people based on outward signs, and therefore were acting as judges with "evil thoughts."

Imagine the heart of Jesus as he considers this reality. He must cry at the idea of your being left outside the assembly. He wants you inside, worshipping God with a joyful heart.

If we look at the last several verses, we get an additional peek at God's heart for the situation. We see that partiality is sinful. And we see that those who hold the Law up as a Holy thing must comply with every last jot and tittle, or be convicted by that very Law.

God wants everyone welcomed to the table, with no partiality driven by clothing, haircut, or gender expression. Those who make others feel uncomfortable or unwelcome are guilty of violating the entire Law.

I was taught that no one gets to stand between you and God, and that you get to make the choice about who you are, about how you will live your life, about whether or not you will follow Jesus. If we can believe that it is up to each individual to make choices of that importance about their souls, can't people also be trusted to make their own choices about their own bodies and identities?

Vivian Taylor

TRANSFORMATION

Deciding to live authentically can be hard and frightening. Each step toward authenticity carries its own joys and sorrows. Take courage in knowing we have a God of transformation and becoming; a God who delights in their creation; a God who wants you to be fully you.

In this focus area, we look at scripture which addresses the idea of transition and transformation.

DAY 27: YOU ARE A NEW CREATION

From now on, therefore, we regard no one from a human point of view; even though we once knew Christ from a human point of view, we know him no longer in that way. So if anyone is in Christ, there is a new creation: everything old has passed away; see, everything has become new! All this is from God, who reconciled us to himself through Christ, and has given us the ministry of reconciliation; that is, in Christ God was reconciling the world to himself, not counting their trespasses against them, and entrusting the message of reconciliation to us. So we are ambassadors for Christ, since God is making his appeal through us; we entreat you on behalf of Christ, be reconciled to God. For our sake he made him to be sin who knew no sin, so that in him we might become the righteousness of God.
(2 Corinthians 5:16-21 NRSV)

Let's read the second sentence again:

So if anyone is in Christ, there is a new creation: everything old has passed away; see, everything has become new!

God is all about transformation. On the mountain top, Jesus was transfigured before three close friends. When he exited the tomb, the beloved woman who'd washed his feet with her tears didn't recognize him. Two men who met him while walking on the road to Emmaus had no idea Jesus was with them.

But Jesus isn't the only one who transforms. He promises each of us that we will be changed in the twinkling of an eye.

Today's passage shows us that this happens for a reason. God doesn't smile on our gender transformation solely because they delight in our being authentic. They also have expectations for our changes; that we be ambassadors of light and reconciliation.

This is a high calling and, at times, a painful one. We may not always be safely able to reconcile with those who can't understand our transitioning. But we can try to be open to it, and seek it where it is possible.

The role of ambassador isn't necessarily easy. As you face confused and sometimes judgmental glances or worse, the temptation to respond with disdain and anger will be strong. But God calls us to shine the light of Christ to the world.

You must be smart. You must be safe. And you must also remember that you are a new creation; you are the righteousness of God.

A Christian is a keyhole through which other folk see God.
Robert E. Gibson

DAY 28: JESUS THE TRANSFIGURED

*About eight days after Jesus said this, he took Peter, John and James with
him and went up onto a mountain to pray. As he was praying, the
appearance of his face changed, and his clothes became as bright as a flash
of lightning. Two men, Moses and Elijah, appeared in glorious splendor,
talking with Jesus. They spoke about his departure, which he was about to
bring to fulfillment at Jerusalem. Peter and his companions were very
sleepy, but when they became fully awake, they saw his glory and the two
men standing with him.*
(Luke 9:28-32 NIV)

Today's passage describes how Jesus is transfigured on a mountaintop
with his closest male disciples present. Don't you wish Luke had offered
more words about this stunning scene, when God shines light from
within Christ so brightly that it changes how he looks, and changes
how those who are watching view him?

Let's look at the word upon which this devotional is based:

Trans·fig·ure: to transform into something more beautiful or
elevated.

When Jesus was transfigured, he was revealed as more fully himself.
More of the truth about him was displayed than had been previously
seen.

Of course Jesus *is* Truth, and the truth has to shine, just as his face
did that day.

When you first began to express gender authentically, did you feel
a tiny bit of that shine of truth? Did part of your spirit sing *Yes!*
amidst the other mix of emotions that were in play?

Let's look at what comes a bit later in this story:

*A voice came from the cloud, saying, "This is my Son, whom I have
chosen; listen to him."* (Luke 9:35 NIV)

Moses and Elijah converse with the luminescent Jesus that day.
They are the human symbols of the Law and the Prophets;
representatives of the Old Covenant and everything which came

before this transformative moment. And the Creator says—to them and to us—to listen to Jesus; the shining light of truth who never dictated gender and who preached a gospel of radically inclusive love.

It wasn't easy for Jesus, despite the affirmation of his father. It won't be easy for you. But God is well pleased with your own effort to shine with truth as you walk in the light of Christ.

> *There is meaning in every journey that is unknown to the traveler.*
> Dietrich Bonhoeffer

DAY 29: LAYING ASIDE THE OLD SELF AND SPEAKING TRUTH

So this I say, and affirm together with the Lord, that you walk no longer just as the Gentiles also walk, in the futility of their mind, being darkened in their understanding, excluded from the life of God because of the ignorance that is in them, because of the hardness of their heart; But you did not learn Christ in this way, if indeed you have heard Him and have been taught in Him, just as truth is in Jesus, that, in reference to your former manner of life, you lay aside the old self, which is being corrupted in accordance with the lusts of deceit, and that you be renewed in the spirit of your mind, and put on the new self, which in the likeness of God has been created in righteousness and holiness of the truth.
(Ephesians 4:17-18, 20-24 NASB)

Paul's letter to the Ephesians calls out unwillingness to accept the Word God offers to the whole world. It's a theme which sounds throughout the New Testament; a dark and twisted thread running through the fabric of otherwise good news. In the gospels we hear stories of fundamentalist religious experts who demand that Jesus is not only wrong in proclaiming love, acceptance, and radical inclusiveness, but that he should be killed for it.

Here's another reading which echoes this theme:

Therefore, since we have such a hope, we are very bold. We are not like Moses, who would put a veil over his face to prevent the Israelites from seeing the end of what was passing away. But their minds were made dull, for to this day the same veil remains when the old covenant is read. It has not been removed, because only in Christ is it taken away. Even to this day when Moses is read, a veil covers their hearts. But whenever anyone turns to the Lord, the veil is taken away. Now the Lord is the Spirit, and where the Spirit of the Lord is, there is freedom. And we all, who with unveiled faces contemplate the Lord's glory, are being transformed into his image with ever-increasing glory, which comes from the Lord, who is the Spirit. (2 Corinthians 3:12-18 NIV)

Rejecting the message of Christ isn't something done solely by the people of Jesus' day. These biblical stories are not mere historical records, they are still in play: a veil covers the hearts of legalistic Christians so they can't read scripture through the lens of Christ's freedom.

Unveiling our faces doesn't show lack of respect for the Law or the Bible. When we, with unveiled faces, contemplate Jesus' mercy, compassion, and loving acceptance we are transformed into his image.

Today's passages point this out, and also speak to those who are transitioning. Jesus calls us to put aside our old lives and to put on new selves; selves of love, freedom, generosity, and the holiness of truth.

Accept the good news. Your authentic self is the very likeness of God. Go spread God's glory with boldness.

Do not wish to be anything but what you are, and try to be that perfectly.
Francis de Sales

DAY 30: GRABBING HOLD OF HIS HEM

But as He went, the multitudes thronged Him. Now a woman, having a
flow of blood for twelve years, who had spent all her livelihood on
physicians and could not be healed by any, came from behind and touched
the border of His garment. And immediately her flow of blood stopped.
And Jesus said, "Who touched Me?" When all denied it, Peter and those
with him said, "Master, the multitudes throng and press You, and You
say, 'Who touched Me?'" But Jesus said, "Somebody touched Me, for I
perceived power going out from Me." Now when the woman saw that she
was not hidden, she came trembling; and falling down before Him, she
declared to Him in the presence of all the people the reason she had touched
Him and how she was healed immediately.

And He said to her, "Daughter, be of good cheer; your faith has made you
well. Go in peace."
(Luke 8:42b-48 NKJV)

Today we read about an unnamed woman whose faith is so great that it manifests itself in tremendous bravery.

The Hebrew view of menstruation in Jesus' day was encumbered with notions of spiritual uncleanliness, enforced isolation, and rituals for purification. Under normal circumstances, women bore the weight of cleanliness requirements just once a month for decades until menopause eventually halted the cycles. But the limits inflicted on this woman didn't let up for twelve straight years.

Observing the Jewish customs meant she would have stayed away from men so she couldn't accidentally touch them and therefore make them also ritually unclean. She was probably looked down upon by her society; disdained for her perpetual flow of blood.

Trans masculine people may feel a special resonance with her, knowing what it it's like to just want the bleeding to stop; spending money and suffering under the processes of transitioning. But all gender-queer people can find a connection with this woman, who endured so much and yet pushed through to grab hold of Jesus. Her culture said she should have stayed away, should have remained hidden so she wouldn't affront anyone's sensibilities. It would have been more comfortable for the religious people around her if they didn't have to recognize the hardship which following the Law inflicted on her; the deprivation of freedom, community, and respect. They would undoubtedly have preferred that she remain sequestered; out of sight, and out of mind.

But this brave, nameless soul broke through the shackles of law. She knew she was violating rules for being out on the street, and for touching countless people in the throngs surrounding Jesus. She knew that touching his cloak would be considered a defilement of a holy man.

A defilement, in fact, of God themself.

In response, Jesus turned to her, called her daughter, and celebrated the power of her faith. He glorified her action rather than condemning it, and he didn't bother to perform the purification ritual which law dictated after their contact.

The woman entered the scene nameless, disdained, and excluded by society. She left it bearing the title "daughter," healed, and knowing she was loved.

This is the power of Christ.

Jesus does not disdain you for the things religious experts say you shouldn't do, be, or feel. Jesus doesn't want you to stay away from him out of some idea that you would sully Christianity by your presence. Jesus wants you to break through the crowd and grab hold of any part of him you can reach.

And when you do, he will claim you as his beloved child.

I live my life knowing that God loves me. I know this because I completely put my fate in His hands, and for doing that I have seen the ultimate result of His unconditional love. In the end, it only matters what He thinks of me, because I know if He loves me then others will, too. This is God's redemption for me.
Rachel Clark

DAY 31: GOD'S DESIRE TO COMFORT US LIKE A MOTHER

If my father and mother forsake me, the Lord will take me up.
(Psalm 27:10 NRSV)

Jesus has a special place in his heart for those who are sorrowing. Just look at the beatitudes in Matthew:

"Blessed are the poor in spirit, for theirs is the kingdom of heaven. Blessed are those who mourn, for they will be comforted. Blessed are those who hunger and thirst for righteousness, for they will be filled. "Blessed are you when people insult you, persecute you and falsely say all kinds of evil against you because of me. (Matthew 5:3-4, 6, 11 NIV)

One of the interesting things about this portion of Jesus' Sermon on the Mount is that it is all present tense. We mostly think about the verses as a promise for the future; and they are, in part. But "blessed" means *now*.

Blessed *are*, the beatitudes say.

It's hard to feel blessed while being insulted and persecuted. Sorrowing over parents, friends, or churches which have rejected you makes it nearly impossible to claim blessedness. And the Lord knows how frequently Christians persecute using God's name.

Jesus assures us of blessing, but that doesn't mean God enjoys your suffering. Today's opening verse is a prayer for you to remember when the pain of family rejection hits. The Lord *will* take you up. Here's another one like it:

"As one whom his mother comforts, so I will comfort you; you shall be comforted in Jerusalem." (Isaiah 66:13 ESV)

God offers comfort in the times that are the hardest, and most lonely. Claim your blessedness. Go to the Holy Spirit in the midst of that pain, and ask her to fulfill these promises of consolation.

Never be afraid to trust an unknown future to a known God.
Corrie ten Boom

DAY 32: TRANSFORMING HEARTS OF STONE

Thus says the Lord God: Because, yea, because they made you desolate,
and crushed you from all sides, so that you became the possession of the rest
of the nations, and you became the talk and evil gossip of the people;
A new heart I will give you, and a new spirit I will put within you; and I
will take out of your flesh the heart of stone and give you a heart of flesh.
And I will put my spirit within you, and cause you to walk in my statutes
and be careful to observe my ordinances. You shall dwell in the land which
I gave to your fathers; and you shall be my people, and I will be your God.
(Ezekiel 36:3, 26-28 RSV)

The prophetic books of the Hebrew Scriptures are filled with examples of the Jewish people turning away from God, repenting, and God's hurry to embrace them.

Perhaps your life experiences caused you to turn away from God in the past. Maybe you're even struggling with it now. When you've been the brunt of religious and social persecution, it can be hard not to be angry with God for permitting it. Pulling away from everything associated with the things which have hurt you so deeply is understandable.

If you've done that, or if you are in the midst of it now and reading this book in hope of re-engaging in active relationship with God, please know that your Creator is waiting like the father of the Prodigal Son. God knows the pain it's caused for your heart to have to be hardened so that you can simply survive.

We have a God of transformation. He knows the times you have been desolate, crushed from all sides, and gossiped about. He sees you, and knows you, and desires freedom and wholeness for you.

As you go through the transitions which permit you to live authentically, remember God's promise in this passage. God is with you in it and through it. They want to create in you a new heart to go along with the other newness you are experiencing. And they want you to remember that you are God's people, and that they are your God.

We are all prisoners but some of us are in cells with windows and some without.
Kahlil Gibran

Day 33: Resurrected Bodies

But someone will ask, "How are the dead raised? With what kind of body will they come?" How foolish! What you sow does not come to life unless it dies. When you sow, you do not plant the body that will be, but just a seed, perhaps of wheat or of something else. But God gives it a body as he has determined, and to each kind of seed he gives its own body. Not all flesh is the same: People have one kind of flesh, animals have another, birds another and fish another. There are also heavenly bodies and there are earthly bodies; but the splendor of the heavenly bodies is one kind, and the splendor of the earthly bodies is another. The sun has one kind of splendor, the moon another and the stars another; and star differs from star in splendor.

So will it be with the resurrection of the dead. The body that is sown is perishable, it is raised imperishable; it is sown in dishonor, it is raised in glory; it is sown in weakness, it is raised in power; it is sown a natural body, it is raised a spiritual body.

If there is a natural body, there is also a spiritual body. So it is written: "The first man Adam became a living being"; the last Adam, a life-giving spirit. The spiritual did not come first, but the natural, and after that the spiritual. The first man was of the dust of the earth; the second man is of heaven. As was the earthly man, so are those who are of the earth; and as is the heavenly man, so also are those who are of heaven. And just as we have borne the image of the earthly man, so shall we bear the image of the heavenly man.
(1Corinthians 15:35-49 NIV)

Fundamentalist Christians seem to be obsessed with bodies, whether it's demanding who shouldn't have sex with whom, or proclaiming what body parts equate to what gender descriptor. Scripture tells us we are made in God's likeness; therefore our bodies must be a reflection of God in some mystical way. So while many people like to think our bodies are meaningless in the eyes of God and for our eternal future, that simply can't be right.

Today's words from Paul point out the gorgeous diversity of the bodies God created, all of which are matter presented in different forms. Matter is nothing but elaborate arrangements of energy manifesting itself in an astonishing array of shapes and sizes. All the shapes are beautiful; from the tiniest bacterium to the most incandescent expanding star. They are also all perishable; destined to lose their current form. But while shapes perish, the energy which comprises those shapes remains.

This is an awe-inspiring reality.

In Romans Paul tells us that we are all one body in Christ. Jesus is the alpha and the omega, the beginning and the end, and through him all things were made including you and I.

We are all made of the same stuff; the glorious energy God created through their ecstatic big bang: you, and I, and the person who tormented you for wearing clothes they thought belonged on someone else. We are *all* the flesh of Jesus himself, all bearer-beings of his Spirit, the Holy She.

Our transitions and becomings are important to our manifestation of truth in our current energy configurations. But even though living our truth is important, remember that our current bodies are holy magnificence which will perish in their current forms so they can transcend and become even more fully the splendor of Christ.

The glorious, splendid best is yet to come for you, beloved manifestation of God.

Do not pray for easy lives; pray to be stronger men. Do not pray for tasks equal to your powers; pray for powers equal to your tasks. Then the doing of your work shall be no miracle, but you yourself shall be a miracle. Every day you shall wonder at yourself, at the richness of life which has come to you by the grace of God.
Phillips Brooks

FREE TO BE

Galatians 5:1 tells us it is for freedom that Jesus set us free, and that we should therefore stand firm and not be burdened again by the yoke of slavery.

As you move at your own pace through the process of becoming free, remember that God doesn't desire for you to be burdened by the yoke of societal expectations for your selfhood. Anyone who tells you otherwise is simply wrong.

Over the next week you'll encounter scriptures designed to encourage your efforts to walk in freedom.

DAY 34: DECLARING THINGS UNCLEAN CREATES STUMBLING BLOCKS

One person's faith allows them to eat anything, but another, whose faith is weak, eats only vegetables. The one who eats everything must not treat with contempt the one who does not, and the one who does not eat everything must not judge the one who does, for God has accepted them. Who are you to judge someone else's servant? To their own master, servants stand or fall. And they will stand, for the Lord is able to make them stand.

You, then, why do you judge your brother or sister? Or why do you treat them with contempt? For we will all stand before God's judgment seat. It is written: "'As surely as I live,' says the Lord, 'every knee will bow before me; every tongue will acknowledge God.'"

So then, each of us will give an account of ourselves to God. Therefore let us stop passing judgment on one another. Instead, make up your mind not to put any stumbling block or obstacle in the way of a brother or sister.
(Romans 14:2-4, 10-13 NIV)

Reading Paul's letters can result in a great deal of confusion. At one moment, he chides churches about things like women wearing gold necklaces, and the next minute offers up glowing words of encouragement and good news. Much of this contrast arises from contextual issues which Paul needed to address. But it's also possible that one of the thorns in Paul's flesh was the siren call of Phariseeism. Details of the law were drilled into him and he was one of the elite holders of all that rigidity. It had to have been challenging for him to negotiate between his years of training and this new thing offered by Christ.

We see that struggle throughout the epistles, and because of it, we need to remember to filter his words through the lens of Jesus. Today's message doesn't need much filtering, because it aligns so closely to what we see Jesus saying and doing throughout the gospels.

Many people today do not understand gender complexity. They've been taught, as Paul was, that God established rules which were more important than compassion, mercy, and justice. They view gender as falling into those rules. Some of these people are more fully able to walk as Christ showed us, and tread gently in this topic. Others are more vocal, more deprecating, and more likely to wield hammers of law.

When you encounter the latter who don't know how to accept your gender identity, expression, or performance, offer them this passage. Tell them you will pray for them to lay down the burden of law which has become a thorn in the very flesh of Christ, and embrace God's freedom.

> *We're not broken. We're not in the wrong bodies. We're not inadequate. We're not lesser. We're not unwanted. We're not fraudulent. We're not undesirable. That's all just a set of lies we tell to soothe the experience of the prisons we put ourselves in.*
>
> Agnostic Zetetic

DAY 35: BREAKING OUT OF PRISON

Now when Herod was about to bring him out, on that very night, Peter was sleeping between two soldiers, bound with two chains, and sentries before the door were guarding the prison. And behold, an angel of the Lord stood next to him, and a light shone in the cell. He struck Peter on the side and woke him, saying, "Get up quickly." And the chains fell off his hands. And the angel said to him, "Dress yourself and put on your sandals." And he did so. And he said to him, "Wrap your cloak around you and follow me." And he went out and followed him. He did not know that what was being done by the angel was real, but thought he was seeing a vision. When they had passed the first and the second guard, they came to the iron gate leading into the city. It opened for them of its own accord, and they went out and went along one street, and immediately the angel left him. When Peter came to himself, he said, "Now I am sure that the Lord has sent his angel and rescued me from the hand of Herod and from all that the Jewish people were expecting."
(Acts 12:6-11 ESV)

Non-binary and transgender people's stories of existence before living authentically evoke prison imagery. Going through life wearing a persona rather than simply *being* makes people feel trapped; imprisoned by the expectations and demands of family, church, and career.

The book of Acts includes several stories of miraculous prison escapes, like the one Peter experienced in today's reading. From it we notice a few things. First is the timing. The chains don't fall away at a time Peter demanded. In fact, he was sleeping when freedom finally came. Second, Peter had to cooperate. He could have stayed where he was, too frightened of potential repercussions to take action. Third, Peter acknowledged that God was on his side and desired his freedom.

While Peter went free as a result of this angelic visitation, that didn't mean everything was smooth sailing afterward. He did great things in the early church, but he was eventually put to death by crucifixion.

We are all bound and stuck in various kinds of prisons. God sends opportunities to exit them in ways large and small, through simple words and magnificent miracles. We need to be attuned to the messages of the Holy Spirit and of angels, whispering in our ears and hearts about when to stay and when to break free. And we need to remember to count the joys of being let out of prison, because there will also be cost.

Peter was called by Jesus to play a profound role in the formation of the church. Jesus calls you for your own role in the body of Christ today. Be alert and attentive for his invitation to freedom so that you can be a unique voice in proclaiming the glory of God.

> *Out of suffering have emerged the strongest souls; the most massive characters are seared with scars.*
> Kahlil Gibran

DAY 36: GOD DOES NOT SHOW FAVORITISM

Glory, honor and peace for everyone who does good: first for the Jew, then for the Gentile. For God does not show favoritism. A person is not a Jew who is one only outwardly, nor is circumcision merely outward and physical. No, a person is a Jew who is one inwardly; and circumcision is circumcision of the heart, by the Spirit, not by the written code. Such a person's praise is not from other people, but from God.
(Romans 2:10-11, 28-29 NIV)

When studying the Bible it doesn't take long to discover what an important role circumcision had in the scriptures. Moses was nearly killed by God for neglecting to circumcise one of his sons; Joshua's band of desert wanderers were circumcised en masse before entering the promised land; and the book of Acts is peppered with mentions of the practice as the young church tried to figure out whether it should be a requirement for gentile believers.

Given the intense connection between the state of one's genitalia and fidelity to God described prior to Jesus' coming, we shouldn't really be surprised that modern-day fundamentalist Christians are still obsessing about it.

Paul tried to set things straight with the leaders of the church in Rome, who wanted to demand that only people who received certain genital surgical procedures could be true believers. He tried to point out that what God wants is something which takes place inside; a spiritual transformation and a new inclination of the heart.

God does not show favoritism. They don't care how your biological sex and your gender identification or performance is manifested. They don't measure your degree of piety based on how much or how little your genitals have been surgically altered. What they care about is how much you love God, your neighbor, and yourself.

Paul's instructions still apply today: Christians are not those who are only Christian outwardly; acting and dressing according to the norms of our denominations and culture. Seek instead to be a Christian as Paul describes in these verses: with your heart circumcised by and into love.

God had thee before he made thee; he loved thee first, and then created thee, that thou loving him, he might continue his love to thee.

John Donne

DAY 37: FORFEITING A LIFE TO GAIN YOURSELF

For whoever wants to save their life will lose it, but whoever loses their life for me will save it. What good is it for someone to gain the whole world, and yet lose or forfeit their very self?
(Luke 9:24-25 NIV)

Deciding to express gender authentically may result in the loss of friends, family, jobs, and roles within church communities. This can be so discouraging that some people change their minds and remain living as their social circle expects because the pain is simply too great. No one wants to lose the life to which they are accustomed, and the prospect of facing such loss at a time when so much is shifting can be overwhelming.

These people need our prayers; that they have discernment about the timing for their transitions, and that they be strengthened and comforted during the waiting. You might even be going through this yourself right now. Please know that people are praying for you.

Prayers are also needed for those whose discomfort and judgement are so strong that it overwhelms their non-binary loved one. May God soften their hearts to receive truth.

The day will eventually come when simply being you won't result in these sorts of losses. Until then, remember that God created you just as you are; uniquely you.

In today's passage, Jesus tells us that retaining the comfort of our normal is not worth the loss of our personhood. When the time is right for your transition, walk with Jesus into your truth, unite the pain of your losses with Christ on the cross, and know that he is saving you.

And if the time isn't yet right, be sure to find ways which honor your truth. God doesn't want you to forfeit the reality of your being.

God is with you as you wait.

Freedom is the open window through which pours the sunlight of the human spirit and human dignity.

Herbert Hoover

DAY 38: FEARFULLY AND WONDERFULLY MADE

Where can I go from your Spirit? Where can I flee from your presence? If I go up to the heavens, you are there; if I make my bed in the depths, you are there. If I rise on the wings of the dawn, if I settle on the far side of the sea, even there your hand will guide me, your right hand will hold me fast. If I say, "Surely the darkness will hide me and the light become night around me," even the darkness will not be dark to you; the night will shine like the day, for darkness is as light to you. For you created my inmost being; knit me together in my mother's womb. I praise you because I am fearfully and wonderfully made; your works are wonderful, I know that full well. My frame was not hidden from you when I was made in the secret place, I was woven together in the depths of the earth. Your eyes saw my unformed body; all the days ordained for me were written in your book before one of them came to be.
(Psalm 139:7-16 NIV)

LGBTQIA+ individuals face a lot of criticism about key issues of identity. Gay, lesbian, and bisexual people just want to be able to love who they love and to whom they are attracted. Transgender people just want to live life according to their true gender. Fundamentalist Christians talk about these things as if they are choices and decisions.

But they aren't.

And you know what? God knows it, even if they don't. They know it because they formed each of us in our mothers' wombs.

As Christians we believe God is in charge of our existence from conception on. As Christians we know God doesn't make mistakes. LGBTQIA+ individuals were formed uniquely and particularly, with all their strengths, weaknesses, inherent skills and talents, physical attributes, and brain power. Just like everyone else. We can take no credit for the fact that we are fast runners, have pretty eyes, are good at math, or have straight teeth. These are all gifts from the God who formed us in the womb. We also can take no credit for our gender or our sexuality, nor can we be condemned for them.

We didn't choose them. God did.

Know you are fearfully and wonderfully made, just as you are. Know you cannot hide who you are from God, nor do you need to. They don't want you to. God is holding you even when you are in darkness, and all your days are written in their book.

God did not create a black and white world of male and female. Creation is not black and white, it is amazingly diverse, like a rainbow, including sexualities and a variety of non-heterosexual expressions of behaviour, affection and partnering occurring in most species, including humans.

Anthony Venn-Brown

DAY 39: CONSECRATED BODIES, RENEWED MINDS

Therefore, I urge you, brothers and sisters, in view of God's mercy, to offer your bodies as a living sacrifice, holy and pleasing to God—this is your true and proper worship. Do not conform to the pattern of this world, but be transformed by the renewing of your mind. Then you will be able to test and approve what God's will is—his good, pleasing and perfect will.
(Romans 12:1-2 NIV)

You are undoubtedly familiar with the pattern of this world, with its rules about what body parts make something male or female, what girls should wear, and how boys should act. You've probably also heard that rigid gender constructs are God's will, and that falling outside of those constructs means disobedience or worse.

Today's verses should be a comfort to you when you hear those messages. Paul tells us something critical about our bodies. He tells us that they are able and worthy of being offered as a sacrifice to God. He also tells us that *we* are in charge of our bodies; no one else has a right to claim that changes to them impacts their ability to be consecrated.

Paul says we should consecrate our minds, which means continually renewing them with the understanding of who it is that created us, loved us, and redeems us.

God is Love.

When you renew that understanding, each and every day, then you can better test what things fall within their good, pleasing, and perfect will.

Consecrate your body to God, for their use and purposes. Renew your mind's understanding that God is Love. When you do these things, you can walk with confidence in your ability to remain within Love's will.

Many Christians think that physical biology is the ultimate truth when we also believe the physical body to be temporary; just a shell for the spirit that will one day pass away. But when it comes to transgender identities, most Christians seem to say, "The brokenness is in the spirit. The body is right. The body is the true identity." But that is not what our theology truly says. We believe that our identity—who we are in Christ—is in the spirit. So for a transgender person, the brokenness would be in the body; a brokenness that could reasonably be treated through therapy, hormone replacement, surgery, or any means available.

Jess Meyer-Crosby

DAY 40: GOD COMES TO SAVE YOU

Say to the fearful of heart:
Be strong, do not fear!
Here is your God,
he comes with vindication;
With divine recompense
he comes to save you.
Then the eyes of the blind shall see,
and the ears of the deaf be opened;
Then the lame shall leap like a stag,
and the mute tongue sing for joy.
(Isaiah 35:4-6 NABRE)

It's not easy to hold up under the emotional strain of listening to arguments about the supposed sinfulness of non-binary and transgender individuals. Sometimes the spiritual blindness and deafness to the cries of pain which traditionalist Christians demonstrate is overwhelming. You may not always know when to speak, or you might think you don't have the right words, or you might just feel outnumbered, and so you remain mute.

But what glorious promises God holds out for us, to encourage us in our efforts both to seek him and to proclaim his love!

In your prayers today, remember these words of encouragement. Pray for that day to come; when the truth shall be laid bare, when blindness and deafness shall be no more. When every tongue which has been bitten until it bleeds to stop from shrieking, instead sings for joy.

Know that the day is coming. Breathe deep, and keep going.

It is frightening to have to trust your own soul. It means you are free, and freedom is terrifying. But here is the thing. We are made in the image of God. We can trust our basic construction. We all need the guidance of a tribe from time to time, but when you are constructed in God's image, your internal locus of control, if you are willing to trust it, will reliably lead you in the direction of the truth. The question is whether or not you will trust it.

Paula Stone Williams

Conclusion

We are at the end of our 40 days of transfiguration together, and in these final words, I remind you of the truth we have explored:

God loves you.

God created you in all your unique beauty, knows you to the breadth of your being, and loves you to your very core.

No part of you is hidden from God's sight. No emotion, no desire for change, no shame or sorrow. God sees it all, and loves you.

Nothing can separate you from that love. No word of scripture, no condemnation by religious authorities, no decision to confirm your body's gender surgically.

Nothing.

Breathe deep of these final words:

> But you are "a chosen race, a royal priesthood, a holy nation, a people of his own, so that you may announce the praises" of him who called you out of darkness into his wonderful light. Once you were "no people" but now you are God's people; you "had not received mercy" but now you have received mercy. (1Peter 2:9-10 NABRE)

You are God's own; chosen, holy, called out of darkness and into mercy. You are the siblings of Jesus Christ; beloved, known, and accepted.

Hear these words. Take them and treasure them as Mary treasured the good news of the child she would bear. May their truth penetrate your heart and mind, and may you go forth to share this good news.

The world needs your particular beauty. My wife and I are in prayer for your journey.

FOR FURTHER STUDY

I considered including resources for those who want to delve deeper into issues related to gender-queer and transgender faith, but organizations change names periodically, new ones are born, and online information sources shift with them. Because of this, I decided it would be more useful to provide links on my website. You can find them here:

http://www.wheretrueloveis.com/resources

Made in the USA
Middletown, DE
12 March 2023

26641105R00060